10/07

FOOTBALL IN THE BIG 12

rosen publishing's
rosen central®

MICHAEL SOMMERS

New York

Published in 2008 by The Rosen Publishing Group, Inc.
29 East 21st Street, New York, NY 10010

Library of Congress Cataloging-in-Publication Data

Football in the Big 12 / Michael Sommers. — 1st ed.
   p. cm. — (Inside college football)
Includes bibliographical references and index.
ISBN-13: 978-1-4042-1921-2 (hardcover)
ISBN-10: 1-4042-1921-8 (hardcover)
1. Big 12 Conference—History.
GV955.5.B54F66 2008
796.332'63—dc22

3 1559 00196 0853

2007007690

Manufactured in the United States of America

On the cover: *(Top)* The Texas A&M Aggies play the University of Kansas Jayhawks in an October 2006 game. *(Bottom)* Cortney Grixby (#2) of the Nebraska Cornhuskers prevents Texas Longhorn Limas Sweed (#4) from scoring a touchdown during the teams' matchup on October 21, 2006.

CONTENTS

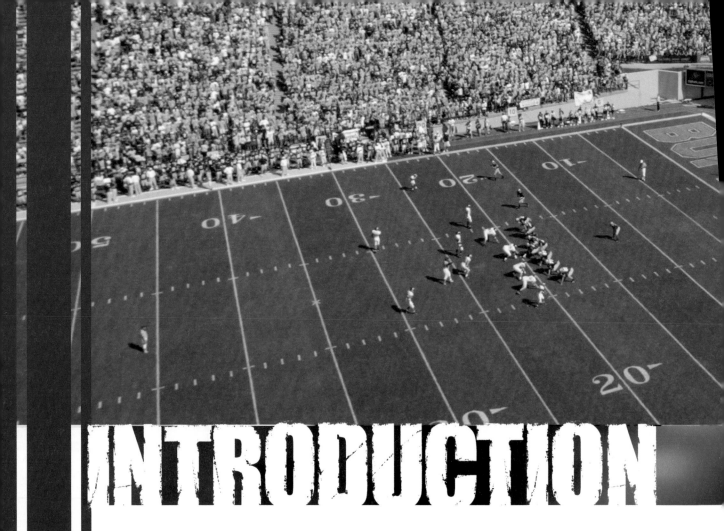

INTRODUCTION

College football is one of the most exciting and popular sports in the United States today. In fact, it was through college games—followed with an almost religious devotion by students, alumni, and local sports fans—that football became one of the most popular sports in America.

The first recorded college football game took place in November 1869 in New Jersey. First-time rivals Princeton and Rutgers played against each other on a gigantic field. The twenty-five members of each team used a round ball and no protective gear. There weren't any officials to referee the game, which was more like soccer than today's football. After Rutgers beat visiting Princeton, the two teams sat down for dinner together, during which Princeton challenged Rutgers to a revenge

On September 3, 2005, a sell-out crowd watches the University of Colorado Buffaloes play in-state rival Colorado State at Folsom Field in Boulder, Colorado.

match. Such was the beginning of one of the biggest athletic pastimes in America.

As new colleges and universities sprouted up across the nation, so did their football teams. Before the invention of film, television, and even radio (not to mention the Internet and DVDs), college football games were among the most exciting and accessible forms of entertainment around. In fact, for decades, college football had a much more passionate following than professional football did. The National Football League (NFL) was created in 1920, but it wasn't until after World War II, which ended in 1945, that professional football became more watched than college games.

However, like pro football, college football has become a big business. Although players themselves aren't paid, they get a lot of attention, particularly since important conference and bowl games are broadcast on network and cable television. Of course, the biggest dream of any college football player is to be recruited by NFL scouts and go on to a professional football career.

College ball is popular particularly in the Midwest and South (home to the Big 12 schools), where campuses are located far from large cities with professional teams. The immense number of fans who show up to root for their teams makes important college games highly profitable. In fact, many major schools have built vast stadiums that seat up to 100,000 people, using benches instead of individual seats in order to fit the growing number of fans. This is especially true with respect to Division I football games.

The division system was invented by the National Collegiate Athletic Association (NCAA), a group that makes up, organizes, and implements rules for most of the collegiate athletic programs in the United States. Division I is considered the highest level of college football; its top teams are split into Division I-A and Division I-AA. Within Division I-A, teams are arranged into twelve different groups called conferences. Teams from each conference are located within the same geographic area and play against each other. Their season generally goes from the end of August through December. At the end of the season, top-ranked teams play each other and against top teams from other conferences in bowl games. The two best teams from all the bowl games compete against each other in the Bowl Champion Series (BCS) National Championship Game.

Although the Big 12 Conference has existed only for ten years, many of its teams have been around for more than a century. Over the years, intense feelings of loyalty as well as rivalries have taken root and grown. As a result, football at these schools is steeped in deep traditions and passions that make Big 12 games some of the most eagerly watched and hotly contested in all college football.

The History of "the Dirty Dozen"

The Big 12 Conference came into being on February 25, 1994. Eight Midwest college teams (which were members of the Big Eight Conference) joined with four Texas schools that had been members of the recently dissolved Southwest Conference.

The first kickoff of the Big 12 took place on August 31, 1996, and pitted the Kansas State Wildcats against the Texas Tech Red Raiders. Among the various opening-game festivities was a skydiver who landed on the field to deliver the first conference ball. Then, in a suspenseful game, the Wildcats defeated the Red Raiders, 21–14.

It took a while for fans to get used to the Big 12. The Big Eight conference, in existence since 1907, had a great many die-hard supporters. In fact, even today, many older fans continue to think of the Big 12 as an enlarged Big Eight. However, soon enough, fans and sportscasters grew enthusiastic about the new conference. As a sign of affection, they began referring to the teams that comprised

A skydiver sails into the Kansas State Wildcats' stadium, preparing to land on the field prior to the start of the first-ever Big 12 game on August 31, 1996.

the Big 12 as "the Dirty Dozen." Meanwhile, as a commercial enterprise, the Big 12 has paid off handsomely. In the first ten years of its existence, it has generated $750 million for its member schools.

See How They Play

The twelve teams that make up the Big 12 Conference are divided into two divisions based on geographical location: the Big 12 North and the Big 12 South. When the Big 12 first began, it was decided that teams would play eight conference games a season. Five of these games would be played against each of the other opponents within the same division. Three would be played against teams from the other division. Games between North and South divisions

A Decade of Big 12 Conference Championship Games

In the first decade of Big 12 Conference Championship Games, several schools have been victors, but none as often as the University of Oklahoma with a total of four wins.

Year	North Division	Score	South Division
1996	Nebraska	27–37	Texas
1997	Nebraska	54–15	Texas A&M
1998	Kansas State	33–36	Texas A&M
1999	Nebraska	22–6	Texas
2000	Kansas State	24–27	Oklahoma
2001	Colorado	39–37	Texas
2002	Colorado	7–29	Oklahoma
2003	Kansas State	35–7	Oklahoma
2004	Colorado	3–42	Oklahoma
2005	Colorado	2–70	Texas
2006	Colorado	7–21	Oklahoma

CURRENT BIG 12 TEAMS AND THEIR ACCOMPLISHMENTS

	SCHOOL	TEAM NAME	COLORS	CONFERENCE CHAMPIONSHIPS	# OF BOWL APPEARANCES	BOWL W–L RECORD
NORTH DIVISION	University of Colorado	Buffaloes	silver, gold, black	1	6	4–2
	Iowa State	Cyclones	cardinal, gold	0	5	2–3
	University of Kansas	Jayhawks	blue, crimson	0	2	1–1
	Kansas State	Wildcats	purple, white	1	8	4–4
	University of Missouri	Tigers	black, old gold	0	4	2–2
	University of Nebraska	Cornhuskers	scarlet, cream	2	9	5–3
SOUTH DIVISION	Baylor	Bears	green, gold	0	0	0–0
	University of Oklahoma	Sooners	crimson, cream	4	7	4–3
	Oklahoma State	Cowboys	orange, purple	0	4	1–3
	University of Texas	Longhorns	orange, white	2	9	4–4
	Texas A&M	Aggies	maroon, white	1	6	1–5
	Texas Tech	Red Raiders	scarlet, black	0	8	3–5

would consist of a "three-on, three-off" system. For instance, each North team would play three South teams for two seasons, before playing the other three South teams for the following two seasons.

Unfortunately, traditional rival teams, which were now in different divisions, would have to wait two years before playing each other. Historically, such competitions had always been particularly fierce among former Big Eight teams, which had been butting heads for decades. Over the years, legendary rivalries had formed between the Nebraska Cornhuskers and the Oklahoma Sooners, for example, as well as between the Oklahoma State Cowboys and the Missouri Tigers. Intense rivalries also had grown between the four Texan

MOST RECENT BOWL APPEARANCE	# OF PLAYERS TO WIN HEISMAN	1ST-ROUND NFL DRAFT PICKS	# OF PLAYERS IN NFL HALL OF FAME	# OF PLAYERS/ COACHES IN NCAA HALL OF FAME
2005 Sports Bowl: Clemson 19, Colorado 10	1	22	0	4
2005 Houston Bowl: Texas Christian University 27, Iowa State 24	0	1	0	0
2005 Fort Worth Bowl: Kansas 42, Houston 13	0	9	3	0
2006 Texas Bowl: Rutgers 37, Kansas State 10	0	4	0	0
2006 Sun Bowl: Oregon State 39, Missouri 38	0	11	1	0
2007 Cotton Bowl: Auburn 17, Nebraska 14	3	31	3	13
1994 Alamo Bowl: Washington State 10, Baylor 3	1	12	1	4
2007 Fiesta Bowl: Boise State 43, Oklahoma 42	4	36	3	0
2007 Independence Bowl: Oklahoma State 34, Alabama 31	1	15	1	0
2006 Alamo Bowl: Texas 26, Iowa 24	2	39	4	0
2006 Holiday Bowl: California 45, Texas A&M 10	1	25	1	0
2006 Insight Bowl: Texas Tech 44, Minnesota 41	0	7	0	0

teams. For decades, under the Big Eight and Southwest Conference, these teams met up at least once during every season. With the Big 12's new rules, players and fans felt cheated. However, when these rivals finally do meet up, the atmosphere at the stadiums is nothing short of explosive.

Championship Games

The top Big 12 team from the South Division plays the top team from the North Division at the end of the season. This highly anticipated final game is known as the Big 12 Championship Game.

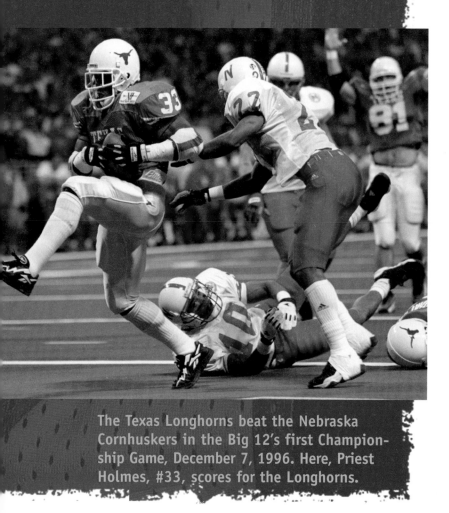

The Texas Longhorns beat the Nebraska Cornhuskers in the Big 12's first Championship Game, December 7, 1996. Here, Priest Holmes, #33, scores for the Longhorns.

The conference champion is assured a place in the prestigious Bowl Championship Series (BCS). The Big 12's first Championship Game was played after the regular 1996 season. The Texas Longhorns beat the Nebraska Cornhuskers 37–27.

Every year, the top eight Big 12 teams are eligible to play in various bowls against other college football champions. The winner is crowned the Division I-A national champ.

Two Big 12 teams have won the BCS Championship Game. In 2000, after a record season of thirteen wins and no losses, Oklahoma defeated Florida State, 13–2, at the Orange Bowl BCS. More recently, in 2005, after an undefeated season and a victory at the Big 12 Conference Championship, the Texas "Horns" beat the top-ranked University of Southern California Trojans. The nail-bitingly close Rose Bowl game ended with a score of 41–38. Many sportswriters have called it one of the best games in college football history.

Legendary Coaches

A great football team is nothing without a great coach. Over the decades, the schools of the future Big 12 would have many outstanding coaches who led them to major victories. Since the Big 12 Conference began in 1996, however, three coaches in particular have captured the attention of football commentators, pros, and fans. They have brought glory to their respective schools, each in their own distinctive way.

Bill Snyder

"Bill Snyder isn't the coach of the year, and he isn't the coach of the decade. He's the coach of the century." These words of praise, published in a 1998 *Sports Illustrated* article by Tim Layden, might seem extravagant on their own. But consider the source: Snyder's

Kansas State coach Bill Snyder talks with his quarterback, Ell Roberson, during the 2004 Fiesta Bowl. The Wildcats suffered a disappointing 35–28 loss against the Ohio State Buckeyes.

biggest *rival*, Barry Switzer. Back in 1998, when Bill Snyder was head coach of the Kansas State Wildcats, Switzer was the coach of one of the Wildcats' biggest rivals, the Oklahoma Sooners. While Oklahoma was considered one of the top college football teams in the nation, until only a few years before, K-State had been considered by *Sports Illustrated* to be "the worst" team in the country. *Sports Illustrated* backed up its claim by referring to K-State's "horrific plays" and "empty bleachers." In fact, in 1988, the Wildcats were so bad that there was talk of expelling them from the Big Eight Conference.

All Work—and All Play

The secret of Bill Snyder's success as a coach was that he was a hard worker. As he told Tim Layden of *Sports Illustrated*: "[My mother] taught me that what the Lord gives you is time, and twenty-four hours a day is all you get." In his years at Kansas State, Snyder's average workday ended around midnight. In addition, he discovered that one could get a lot done during lunch hour. So during football season, he ate only one meal a day, late at night when he got home.

Of course, Snyder didn't confine his hard-work strategy to himself: he demanded it from others as well. While most coaches script (write out plays and strategies) their practices, Snyder scripted his game days and staff meetings, too. Moreover, he expected his assistant coaches to do the same. He also demanded a lot from his players, both on the field and off. On the field, this meant that they practiced more than three hours every day, longer than almost any other team in the country. Off the field, this included being so disciplined that they had to wipe their feet before entering the K-State athletic complex. Snyder even demanded a lot from the school's administrators. He wanted higher salaries for assistant coaches, more money for recruiting players, and renovation of the football complex, which was commonly viewed as a dump. When there was no money to renovate the stadium, Snyder offered to donate a personal check for $100,000!

Luckily for players and fans alike, 1988 was the year that Kansas State decided to hire Bill Snyder to coach its ailing football team. Snyder had started out coaching the University of Southern California (USC) Trojans. He then moved to North Texas State and the University of Iowa before arriving at K-State. Snyder certainly had his work cut out for him. He inherited a twenty-seven-game losing streak and a team that in four seasons had won only three out of forty-four games.

Five years after Snyder arrived at K-State, the Wildcats were the most improved team in American college football. Ten years later, during the 1998 season, the Wildcats were undefeated 11–0. That year, Kansas State shocked the football world by earning its first-ever number-one ranking in the national polls.

During Snyder's seventeen years as head coach at K-State, the Wildcats won more games than they ever had before. Between 1993 and 2003, his coaching led the team to eleven consecutive bowl games, six of which they won. He helped them win four Big 12 North championship titles. In 2003, for the first time ever, the Wildcats won the Big 12 Championship. Two years later, in 2005, Snyder retired from Kansas State. However, he remains responsible for the greatest turnaround in the history of college football. The day after he announced he was leaving, Kansas State renamed its football stadium the Bill Snyder Family Stadium in his honor.

Bob Stoops

During his time at K-State, Bill Snyder hired an assistant coach named Bob Stoops. A former defensive back from the University of Iowa and the son of a coach himself, Stoops joined K-State in 1988. An expert at coaching defense, he played a significant role in the

Coach Bob Stoops of the Oklahoma Sooners congratulates his team during a game against the Texas A&M Aggies on November 9, 2002.

Wildcats' miraculous turnaround. In 1995, Stoops left Kansas State for the University of Florida. Working as defense coordinator, he transformed the Gators into national champions and made himself into one of America's hottest coaches. Suddenly everyone wanted Stoops as their head coach, but it was the University of Oklahoma that got him.

Oklahoma certainly needed him. By the time Stoops came aboard in 1999, the Sooners hadn't had a winning season in several years. A natural leader who excels at bringing out the best in players, Stoops transformed this losing streak—and the team itself—virtually overnight. Under Stoops's guidance, the Sooners

After the Texas Longhorns' thrilling last-minute victory over the University of Southern California Trojans in the 2006 Rose Bowl, a triumphant Mack Brown holds up the National Championship trophy.

had a miraculous 2000 season. Undefeated in thirteen straight games, they then went on to win the BCS National Championship. This spectacular feat was no one-shot deal. The Sooners also made it to the BCS National Championships in 2003 and 2004. Although they didn't win these games, they did capture four Big 12 Conference Championships—in 2000, 2002, 2004, and 2006. In doing so, they became the winningest of all the Big 12 teams, and Stoops gained a reputation as the winningest of all coaches. As a result, other colleges and even NFL teams have repeatedly tried to lure him away from Oklahoma. But to date, Stoops has refused all of these offers, preferring to stay at this highly traditional football school, where being head coach is one of the most desired jobs in all of Division I football.

Mack Brown

At the end of 1997, when Mack Brown was hired as head coach at the University of Texas in Austin, the Longhorns hadn't won a national championship since 1970. Before coming to Texas, Brown had been head coach at the University of North Carolina (UNC). Although under his leadership the UNC Tar Heels had become one of the top-ranked teams in the country, they had failed to win any major conference or national championship games.

During the first few years of the "Brown Era" at Texas, fans and sportscasters complained that Brown's effect on the Longhorns was the same as it had been for the Tar Heels. They nicknamed him "Coach February," claiming that he was great at recruiting new players from high schools (recruiting for college football occurs in February), but failed to follow up with important wins later on in the year. Indeed, during his first five seasons as a coach, Brown was unable to lead the Longhorns to a Big 12 or national championship title (although they did finish in the top ten in 2001 and 2002). Instead, Texas was consistently eliminated by Oklahoma, one of its traditional rivals. However, the 2004 season changed all that.

The year 2004 saw many firsts for the Longhorns. It was the first time they played in the Bowl Championship Series, by qualifying for the 2005 Rose Bowl. It was the first time they played against the Big Ten conference's top-ranked University of Michigan. It was also the first time they won the BCS, thanks to a film-worthy last-second field goal kick by Dusty Mangum. The field goal led the Longhorns to an unexpected victory against Michigan's Wolverines, with a final score of 38–37. The win was also the first time in the Rose Bowl's 103-year history that a game had been decided on the closing play. As a result of the Longhorns' stellar performance, three of their players—Cedric Benson, Derrick Johnson, and Bo Scaife—were drafted by the NFL.

Going into the 2005 season, the Longhorns were ranked as the number-two team in America. But after a nineteen-game winning streak, they ended up number one—twice! First they won the Big 12 Conference championship, crushing the Colorado Buffaloes, 70–3. Then, led by star quarterback Vince Young, they returned to the Rose Bowl. Pitted against the top-ranked USC Trojans, they once again came from behind. With only two minutes left in the game, they scored. The thrilling 41–38 victory made them the 2005 NCAA national champions. It was more than clear that Mack Brown's recruiting had paid off handsomely. Finally, he had succeeded in silencing his former critics. In recognition of his efforts, Brown received the prestigious Paul "Bear" Bryant Award for best coach of 2006.

3 CHAPTER

Major Rivalries

There are many great games in the history of college football and everybody has their favorite moments, plays, and memories. But what really distinguishes college football from professional football, and every other sport for that matter, are the intense rivalries. From large universities to smaller colleges, all schools have their particular rivalries with unique histories—some of which have been going on for more than a century. They transform an other-wise routine game into a much-anticipated revenge match with high emotional stakes. In these cases, rooting against the other team can feel as good as cheering for your own!

The Big 12 teams have some particularly serious football battles that grab the attention not only of students and alumni but of sports fans across the nation. Most of the rivalries existed before the Big 12 Conference formed. The Texas Oklahoma rivalry, especially, has been an intense one for decades. Long before the two schools

In the Lone Star Showdown on November 28, 1940, the University of Texas's Pete Layden (#11) scored the game's only touchdown. The Longhorns defeated the Aggies, 7–0, ending Texas A&M's nineteen-game winning streak.

were in the same conference, they met up on the field for an annual showdown.

In-State Rivalry

In the world of college football, rivalries between schools from the same state can be fierce. In the case of the Big 12, there are several major rivalries that go back for decades. For example, every year since 1911, the University of Kansas and Kansas State have gone head-to-head in the Sunflower Showdown (Kansas is known as "the sunflower state"). The University of Oklahoma and Oklahoma State also have sparred for decades in the Bedlam Series. However, no competition stirs up more passions than the Lone Star Showdown between the University of Texas and Texas A&M. While Longhorns tend to look down on Aggies as simple hicks who couldn't get into U of Texas, Aggies think Longhorns are unbearably snobby. So when the teams meet up, as they have been doing since 1894, they know that the eyes of all of Texas are upon them.

Over the years, Texas has won sixty-seven of these annual matchups, while A&M has racked up thirty-four victories. If you ask Aggies what their greatest game was, they will say the 1939 game in which they beat the Longhorns by a satisfying 20–0. Old Longhorn fans usually recall the game played the following year as their favorite. In 1940, the Longhorns wreaked revenge upon the Aggies

Invented Rivalries

A few college football rivalries are not the result of decades of matchups but are the more recent fruits of pure inventiveness. One notable example is the rivalry dreamed up by University of Colorado Buffaloes' coach Bill McCartney when he first arrived at the school in 1982. Out of the blue, he decided to make the Nebraska Cornhuskers into the Buffs' main rival. He had game schedules printed up with the games against the Huskers highlighted in red ink. McCartney even visited student dorms, trying to coax Colorado students into a competitive frame of mind. Although twenty-five years later, this rivalry is not nearly as intense as others in the Big 12, a certain degree of competitive spirit has developed among some fans.

Proof of this rivalry is a story told by Nebraska fan Jacky Conrad, quoted on ESPN.com's Page 2. She was shopping for food in Boulder, Colorado, before a big Huskers-Buffaloes game. When she came out of the store with her groceries, Conrad was shocked to see that her car was being towed away. It turned out that the store manager had seen her Nebraska license plates and decided that he didn't want a Nebraska car in his parking lot. Commented a shocked Conrad, "I wasn't even wearing my red yet!"

On October 7, 2006, fans watch and cheer during the much-anticipated annual Red River Rivalry game between traditional rivals Texas and Oklahoma. The Longhorns won the game, defeating the Sooners, 28–10.

7–0, ending A&M's nineteen-game winning streak. They proceeded to win against the Aggies thirty-one times over the next thirty-five years.

Cross-Border Conflicts

Some of the most exciting college football games are those between schools from neighboring states. Among the Big 12 teams, there are several particularly intense cross-border rivalries, including Nebraska vs. Oklahoma, and Kansas vs. Missouri. In fact, the latter is known as the "Border War," or the "Border Showdown." It has its roots in the actual border wars between the two states that led to the outbreak of the U.S. Civil War (1861–1865). Today's conflicts on the football field are not nearly as serious, but they are nonetheless quite gripping. After a total of 115 games played, Kansas and Missouri are tied with fifty-three wins each.

Then there is the Red River Rivalry (formerly known as the Red River Shootout), which brings together two football giants: the Texas Longhorns and the Oklahoma Sooners. In existence since 1900, the rivalry is considered one of the greatest in all sports. Its name comes from the Red River, which is a partial boundary between the states. To players and fans, it has the same importance as a conference or national championship game. It is a very emotional rivalry due to historic border disputes as well as economic and cultural differences between the two states. Recently, however, the atmosphere has become even more charged. Although the Longhorns currently lead the series 57–39, losses to Oklahoma from 2000 to 2004 prevented them from playing in the Big 12 Championship Game. Even the states' governors get caught up in the annual fervor! They often place bets, such as having the losing governor present the winning one with a side of beef (this is cattle country after all), which is then donated to charity.

4 CHAPTER

Star Players

Football is a team effort. However, there are always athletes of exceptional ability. They thrill us with their lightning speed, quick thinking, bravado, and personal charisma. Many go on to succeed on professional teams. Since the formation of the Big 12, quite a few stars have been born.

Ricky Williams

One of the Big 12's first star players, the University of Texas's Ricky Williams appeared soon after the formation of the conference. Born in California in 1977, Williams grew up very shy and suffering from an anxiety disorder. However, neither was an obstacle in his developing into a tremendous athlete who was skilled at both baseball and football. In fact, Williams was drafted by baseball's Philadelphia Phillies. He preferred to focus on football, though, and accepted a football scholarship to UT in the fall of 1995. At the age of twenty-one, the six-foot, 225-pound running back became known as "the Texas Tornado."

He earned this nickname in 1998 by setting a NCAA career rushing record with 6,279 yards. That same year, he also broke the NCAA Division I-A career records for rushing touchdowns (73) and scoring (452). Williams's phenomenal performance on the field earned him the prestigious Heisman Trophy. It also caught the attention of the NFL. He was drafted by the New Orleans Saints in 1999. In fact, the Saints' head coach, Mike Ditka, wanted Williams so badly that he traded all of the other draft picks in order to get him—an NFL first!

By the end of his college career, Ricky Williams held twenty NCAA records. Here, he runs upfield in a game against Texas Tech, on November 14, 1998.

Josh Heupel

Oklahoma's quarterback hero was a soft-spoken, exceptionally modest football coach's son from South Dakota named Josh Heupel. What made him one of the nation's best quarterbacks during the two seasons (1999–2001) that he played for the Sooners wasn't his brawn but his brains. In the space of eighteen games, he accumulated twenty-one school and conference passing records. He also helped lead the Sooners to an undefeated regular season, followed by a National Championship victory over Florida State in the 2000 Orange Bowl. Suddenly, the Sooners were the third-best-ranked college football team in the country. In his sixteen years of coaching, Bob Stoops said he had never seen such a dedicated player, let alone such an intelligent one. Heupel's teammates were so impressed with his smarts and leadership qualities that only a few weeks after he joined the Sooners, they elected him team captain.

After being drafted by the Miami Dolphins in 2001, Heupel played in the NFL before returning to Oklahoma in 2004. Having come full circle, Heupel is currently the quarterback coach for the Sooners.

Eric Crouch

One of Josh Heupel's biggest rivals was Eric Crouch, a six-foot-one, 200-pound quarterback from Omaha, Nebraska. In 1999, Frank Solich, the Nebraska Huskers coach, summoned Crouch to substitute for injured quarterback Bobby Newcombe. After five games, Solich put the recovered Newcombe back in. Crouch was so devastated that he drove home to Omaha and contemplated quitting the team.

Solich wasn't about to lose the Cornhuskers' most promising new player. The coach drove to Omaha and convinced Crouch to return. Shortly after, Newcombe was benched and Crouch was calling signals. Remembers Solich, in a *Sports Illustrated* article published in December 2001, "[Crouch was] very much a team player. He understood he was going to be an integral part of what we were going to do at Nebraska." Indeed, soon after, Crouch was racking up the records. He became the Big 12's all-time record holder for total offense with 7,915 yards. He was also one of only three quarterbacks in Division I-A history to rush for 3,000 yards and pass for 4,000 yards in a career. Crouch won his share of prestigious awards, including the 2001 Davey O'Brien Award and the 2001 Heisman Trophy. During each of his three years at the helm of Nebraska's offense, he guided the Cornhuskers into the national top ten. In crucial situations, he always came through, even though prior to entering his final season he had to have surgery twice on his throwing shoulder. Upon graduation, he was drafted by the St. Louis Rams.

Jason White

At the start of the new millennium, the state of Oklahoma was rich in quarterbacks. While Oklahoma State had Eric Crouch, the University of Oklahoma had Jason White. Not only was White an amazing quarterback, but he was also an example of courage and determination. In 1999, he was recruited from his Tuttle, Oklahoma, high school to play with the Sooners. However, he had little time to strut his stuff on the field. Suffering from a series of torn ligaments, he was forced to undergo painful knee surgery in both 2001 and 2002.

Instead of dropping out of football, White was determined to make a comeback. He did so with a vengeance in 2003. He led the Sooners to twelve straight victories and a national championship game in the Sugar Bowl. Having thrown an impressive forty touchdown passes, he also collected an amazing series of awards. These included the Associated Press Player of the Year, Big 12 Offensive Player of the Year, the Davey O'Brien Award, the Jim Thorpe Courage Award, and the coveted Heisman Trophy. White followed up his stellar 2003 performance with another great year. He once again took the Sooners to a national championship game and only narrowly missed winning a second Heisman award. When he graduated in 2004, White was Oklahoma's all-time leader in career passing yards (7,768) and touchdown passes (79).

Adrian Peterson

When Jason White took the Sooners to the national championship in 2004, he had some significant help from star running back Adrian Peterson. A native of Palestine, Texas, Peterson already had gained fame as one of the best high school running backs Texas had ever seen. Unsurprisingly, most college scouts ranked him as the top recruit in America. Although everybody was after him, it was Oklahoma that got him. During his first year with the Sooners,

Big 12 Award Winners

The following is a list of some of the Big 12 athletes who have won national awards. While there are many other awards given away each year, the ones mentioned here are a few of the most prestigious.

Heisman Trophy: Awarded to the most outstanding college football player

Year	Player	School
1998	Ricky Williams (RB)	Texas
2001	Eric Crouch (QB)	Nebraska
2003	Jason White (QB)	Oklahoma

Butkus Award: Awarded to the top linebacker

Year	Player	School
2001	Rocky Calmus (LB)	Oklahoma
2003	Teddy Lehman (LB)	Oklahoma
2004	Derrick Johnson (LB)	Texas

Bronko Nagurski Award: Awarded to the best defensive player

Year	Player	School
2004	Derrick Johnson (LB)	Texas
2003	Derrick Strait (DB)	Oklahoma
2001	Roy Williams (DB)	Oklahoma

Vince Lombardi Award: Awarded to the best lineman (offensive or defensive)

Year	Player	School
1997	Grant Wistrom(DE)	Nebraska
1998	Dat Nguyen (LB)	Texas A&M
2003	Tommie Harris (DT)	Oklahoma

Peterson didn't disappoint. He broke multiple NCAA freshman rushing records with his impressive 1,925 yards. He also led the nation in carries with 339, and he was a finalist for the Heisman Trophy.

Peterson continued to be the talk of OU—and of college football fans everywhere—until a fateful game in October 2006 between Oklahoma and Iowa State. Although the Sooners beat the Cyclones, Peterson broke his collarbone while diving into the end zone after a fifty-three-yard touchdown run. Unable to play for the

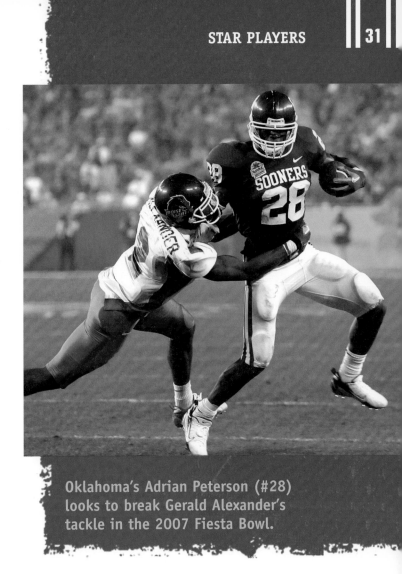

Oklahoma's Adrian Peterson (#28) looks to break Gerald Alexander's tackle in the 2007 Fiesta Bowl.

rest of the season, he returned for the Sooners' final game against Boise State in the 2007 Fiesta Bowl. Peterson performed impressively, rushing for seventy-seven yards. However, Oklahoma just missed winning the game. Instead, Boise edged ahead with a score of 43–42. Despite his injuries, Peterson is still so hot that NFL recruiters are after him to trade his senior year for a trip to the pros.

Vince Young

A prime example of Texas Longhorns' head coach Mack Brown's recruiting talent is powerhouse quarterback Vince Young. A Houston

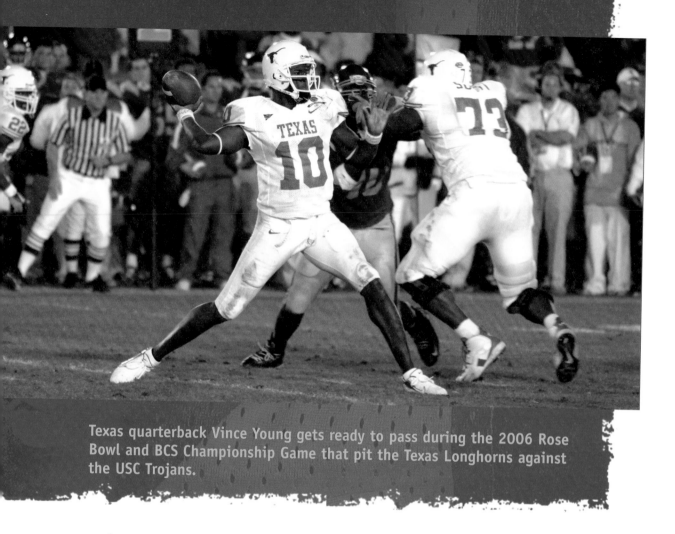

Texas quarterback Vince Young gets ready to pass during the 2006 Rose Bowl and BCS Championship Game that pit the Texas Longhorns against the USC Trojans.

native, Young had a rough childhood. When he was seven, he was hit by a car while riding his bike. The bike's handlebar went into his stomach, nearly killing him. According to Young, the months in the hospital transformed him into a "tougher" individual—a trait that has made him a fearsome opponent on the football field.

After Young's successful high school football career, Brown University recruited him in 2002. After developing and honing his skills, Young was ready to show his determination by his sophomore year. During the 2004 season, he started every game and led the Longhorns to an 11–1 season record, a top-five final ranking, and the school's first-ever Rose Bowl victory, against the University of

Michigan. By this time, he had earned a reputation as a dual-threat quarterback, capable of advancing the ball by passing or rushing.

The 2004 season turned out to be merely a warm-up for Young. In 2005, he led the Longhorns to an undefeated 11–0 regular season, by the end of which they were ranked number two in the nation. The Horns went on to win the Big 12 Championship Game, earning them a spot in the National Championship Rose Bowl against the USC Trojans.

Going into the Rose Bowl game, it seemed unlikely that the Longhorns would win. Sportscasters were touting the Trojans as the greatest football team of all time, thanks in part to the presence of two Heisman Trophy winners. Unfazed by his opponents, Young put on one of the most thrilling individual performances in college football history: 200 yards of rushing, 600 of passing, and three rushing touchdowns. The Longhorns upset the Trojans, winning at the last minute, 41–38. The Longhorns' unexpected triumph, coupled with Young's stunning performance, made him an instant hero. Sportscasters began hailing him the best quarterback ever to have played college football. Even Trojans' coach Pete Carroll was in awe, telling *Sports Illustrated* on January 5, 2006, "That was the best [performance] I've ever seen by one guy."

Unsurprisingly, the NFL scouts came calling. Instead of completing his senior year at the University of Texas, Young was drafted by the Tennessee Titans as their starting quarterback.

5 CHAPTER

Beloved Mascots

College football just wouldn't be the same without a mascot to rally around. The Big 12 teams' mascots are sacred to their fans. Some are live animals. Others are humans dressed up as animals. Still others are humans dressed as mythical figures that represent the school's or state's traditions. No college football game would be complete without the mascots' presence, no matter what form they take.

Live Animals

Since many football teams are named after animals known for their bravery, strength, cunning, and speed, the same animals often become the schools' mascots. In the case of several Big 12 colleges, these mascots are real, live, and much-loved furry beasts.

For example, the Baylor Bears' mascot is an actual bear. The bear is named Judge, in honor of Judge Robert Emmett Bledsoe

Baylor, who gave his name to the Texas university. A local Waco businessman donated the first of Baylor's many Judges in 1917, after winning the bear in a poker game. Traditionally, the Baylor University Chamber of Commerce has been responsible for all care, upkeep, and training of the bears. Currently, there are two North American black bears on campus: Judge Joy Reynolds and Judge Sue Sloan (they are affectionately known as Joy and Lady, respectively). Until the 1990s, the bears were fed Dr Pepper (which was originally made in Waco). However, since the sugar in the soda is bad for the bears' teeth, this "treat" has been suspended. The bears' presence at games is never certain and depends on a variety of factors, including the weather, number of fans present, and the bears' moods on the day of the game.

Another live mascot is Ralphie, the buffalo that represents the Colorado Buffaloes. Ralphie leads the football onto the field at the beginning of both the first and second halves of the game. The original Ralphie appeared in 1934, three weeks after a college contest decided on "Buffaloes" as the team's nickname. A group of students paid $25 to rent a buffalo calf—and his cowboy keeper—for the last game of the season. This first Ralphie was quite excitable: it took the cowboy *and* four students to keep him under control on the sidelines. Today's Ralphie is actually Ralphie IV. Aside from Ralphie, the Buffs have a costumed buffalo mascot known as Chip.

Reveille, a collie, is Texas A&M's live mascot. She is known as the "first lady" of A&M. The original Reveille was a small, poorly nourished black-and-white dog that some students found as a stray. They smuggled her into the dorms to take care of her, but early the next morning, her presence was discovered when she barked during the morning *reveille*, which is French for "wake-up call." Although

Flanking their trusty mascot, Ralphie, members of the Colorado Buffaloes run onto the field before a 1997 game against the Nebraska Cornhuskers.

it was against the rules to keep pets in dorms, the students fell in love with the dog, and she became the school mascot. The current Reveille is actually Reveille VII. Reveilles I–VI are buried in front of the football field, facing the scoreboard (so they can watch the Aggies defeat their opponents).

Reveille isn't the only live-animal college mascot in Texas. Players and fans are fiercely proud of Bevo, the longhorn steer with burnt-orange coloring that honors the University of Texas's team name and colors. The original Bevo was purchased in 1916 to replace the previous (and less obvious) mascot, a bulldog named Pig. The shape of the longhorn's horns inspired the hand symbol

In the stands, fans can be seen making the "Hook 'Em Horns" hand gesture as Bevo, the Longhorns' mascot, looks fierce at a Texas-Oklahoma matchup that took place on October 7, 2006.

and chant "Hook 'Em Horns," which can be seen and heard at all Texas games. The Longhorns' current Bevo is the fourteenth in a long line of Longhorn mascots. Aside from his usual football duties, Bevo attended President George W. Bush's second inauguration in January 2005.

Humans Dressed as Animals

In 1922, a bobcat named Touchdown served as the Kansas State Wildcats' original team mascot. However, keeping Touchdown in a cage all the time was a little depressing. So in 1947, along came

During a 2006 game between the Missouri Tigers and the Kansas Jayhawks, Missouri's mascot, Truman the Tiger, takes a break.

Willie Wildcat. The first Willie was a high school gymnast who dressed up in a brown wildcat costume. Later Willies all have been college students whose identities are kept secret. Since being Willie for a few hours can be very hot, the head of Willie's costume includes an internal electronic cooling fan.

Although the University of Missouri's costumed mascot is a tiger, it wasn't named after the great Asian cat. Instead the name honors a historic group of brave Missouri citizens. The nickname "Tigers" goes back to the Civil War period of the 1860s. At that time, bandits often raided small Missouri towns. To defend themselves, townspeople created companies of home guards. One such company, called the Missouri Tigers, gained a reputation for exceptional bravery. Missouri's football team, created in 1890, therefore became known as "Tigers." Truman the Tiger also pays homage to a U.S. president. His first name honors Missouri-bred Harry S. Truman.

Another mascot that has its origins in Civil War–era history is the Kansas Jayhawk. A mythical bird, the jayhawk is a cross between a blue jay and a sparrow hawk. A Kansan cavalry regiment adopted the term, calling themselves "Jayhawkers." It came to be associated with brave Kansans fighting for an independent state. When, in 1861, Kansas was admitted to the United States as a free state, all Kansans became known as Jayhawkers. In addition, the Jayhawk became the symbol of the University of Kansas. On the field, the Jayhawks are represented by two costumed blue-and-crimson mascots: the bigger (and tougher) Big Jay, and the smaller (and cuter) Baby Jay.

One of the most complicated mascots ever dreamed up was that of the cyclone, for the Iowa State Cyclones. After all, how exactly does one go about dressing up as a swirling tunnel of wind? In the early 1950s, Iowa State's sports director Harry Burrell attempted to build a stuffed costume that would somewhat resemble a column of wind. When his failed, a student competition was held to come up with a more practical mascot. The winning idea was a cardinal based on the school's colors of cardinal and gold. All the red bird needed was a name. Another contest was held, and Cy was born.

In the mascot's early years, students from rival schools often stole the Cy costume before games and held it for ransom. These days, Cy is more carefully guarded. So are the identities of the four to six Iowa State students who play the role of Cy each year.

Lil' Red, one of the Nebraska Cornhuskers' mascots, interacts with the fans at a 2002 game against the Kansas State Wildcats.

Folk Figures

Several of the Big 12 teams' mascots are legendary human beings that have historical significance. In some cases, schools have more than one mascot.

The University of Nebraska Cornhuskers started off with one mascot, named Herbie Husker. A big fan favorite, Herbie drives around the football field in a football-helmet-shaped golf cart. More recently, Herbie gained a sidekick of an inflatable eight-foot doll named Lil' Red. (Lil' Red filled in for him when he was getting a makeover in 2003 and has stayed around ever since.)

Texas Tech is another college with two mascots: the Masked Rider and Raider Red. The Masked Rider is the older of the two. Originally known as "the Ghost Rider," this unofficial mascot first appeared in 1936 when, during home games, an unknown student would ride onto the field on horseback and then gallop away. Renamed the Masked Rider, this black-outfitted rider (only the inside of his cape is red) on a black horse became the official mascot in 1954. Later, when a rule prohibited bringing live-animal mascots to away games, a Wild West cowboy character named Raider Red was created. The identity of the student who dresses up as Raider Red is kept secret.

Going Strong

It has been a little more than ten years since an entire conference and half of another one joined together—amid plenty of doubts— to become the Big 12. The doubters, however, had nothing to fear. As the conference enters its second decade, there are talented coaches and players, exciting team rivalries, and the promise of many more thrilling games to come. It's true that many elements of Big 12 football, from the age-old rivalries to much-loved mascots, continue to make it one of the most fiercely traditional of all college football conferences. Updated technology and up-and-coming talent also have breathed new life into the Big 12, resulting in its games being some of the most eagerly watched throughout the United States. If the past decade's gains in popularity and profitability are any indication, the Big 12 will continue to grow in the years to come.

FOR MORE INFORMATION

Big 12 Conference
400 East John Carpenter Freeway
Irving, TX 75062
(469) 524-1000
Web site: http://www.big12sports.com

College Football Hall of Fame
111 South St. Joseph Street
South Bend, IN 46601
(800) 440-FAME (3263)
Web site: http://www.collegefootball.org

National Collegiate Athletic Association (NCAA)
700 W. Washington Street
P.O. Box 6222
Indianapolis, IN 46206-6222
(317) 917-6222
Web site: http://www.ncaa.org/wps/portal

Web Sites

Due to the changing nature of Internet links, Rosen Publishing has developed an online list of Web sites related to the subject of this book. This site is updated regularly. Please use this link to access the list:

http://www.rosenlinks.com/icf/fb12

FOR FURTHER READING

Bradley, Michael. *Big Games: College Football's Greatest Rivalries*. Dulles, VA: Potomac Books, 2006.

MacCambridge, Michael. *ESPN College Football Encyclopedia*. New York, NY: ESPN Books, 2005.

Nichols, John. *Big Red! The Nebraska Cornhuskers' Story* (College Football Today). Mankato, MN: Creative Education, 1999.

Ours, Robert M. *Bowls: College Football's Greatest Tradition*. Yardley, PA: Westholme Publishing, 2004.

Smith, Steve. *Forever Red: Confessions of a Cornhusker Football Fan*. Lincoln, NE: University of Nebraska Press, 2005.

Whittingham, Richard. *Rites of Autumn: The Story of College Football*. New York, NY: Free Press, 2001.

Wolfe, Jason, and Stephanie Wolfe. *Autumn's Cathedrals: A Pictorial Tour of Division 1-A Football Stadiums*. Roseville, CA: Publishers Design Group. 2002.

BIBLIOGRAPHY

"Casting Crouch." SportsIllustrated.com. December 8, 2001. Retrieved January 2007 (http://sportsillustrated.cnn.com/football/college/2001/heisman/news/2001/12/08/crouch_heisman_ap).

College Football Encyclopedia. "Introduction: A Brief History of College Football." Retrieved January 2007 (http://www.footballencyclopedia.com/cfeintro.htm).

Drehs, Wayne. "Heupel on Biggest Stage of His Life." ESPN.com. October 26, 2000. Retrieved January 2007 (http://espn.go.com/ncf/s/heupel.html).

Huskers.com. "Football." Retrieved January 2007 (http://www. huskers.com/SportSelect.dbml?DB_OEM_ID=100&KEY=&SPID= 22&SPSID=3).

Jones, Bomani. "Why Are Rivalries So Intense?" ESPN Page 2. Retrieved January 2007 (http://sports.espn.go.com/espn/ page2/story?page=jones/050902&num=0).

Kerkhoff, Blair. "League of Its Own." *Kansas City Star*, June 17, 2006. Retrieved January 2007 (http://www.kansascity.com/ mld/kansascity/sports/colleges/big_12_conference/ 14839335.htm).

K-StateSports.com. "Football." Retrieved January 2007 (http://www. kstatesports.com/SportSelect.dbml?DB_OEM_ID=400&KEY= &SPID=212&SPSID=3065).

Layden, Tim. "Miracle Worker." *Sports Illustrated*. November 9, 1998. Posted on DDY's Cats Page. Retrieved January 2007 (http:// www.ddy.com/catsfb_miracle.html).

Mack Brown. "Texas Football." Retrieved January 2007 (http://www. mackbrown-texasfootball.com).

Mandel, Stewart. "Running His Way into History." Inside College Football. SportsIllustrated.com. January 5, 2006. Retrieved January 2007 (http://sportsillustrated.cnn.com/2006/ writers/stewart_mandel/01/05/rose.young/index.html).

SoonerSports.com. "Football." Retrieved January 2007 (http://www. soonersports.com/SportSelect.dbml?DB_OEM_ID=300&KEY= &SPSID=2475).

INDEX

About the Author

Michael A. Sommers was born in Texas and raised in Canada. After earning a bachelor's degree in English literature at McGill University in Montreal, Canada, he went on to complete a master's degree in history and civilizations from the École des Hautes Études en Sciences Sociales in Paris, France. For the last fifteen years, Sommers has worked as a writer and photographer. He lives in Brazil, where football—of another type—is a national passion.

Photo Credits

Cover top, bottom, pp. 12, 14, 17, 24, 31 © Getty Images; pp. 1, 3 © www.istockphotos.com/Stefan Klein; pp. 4–5 © Icon SMI; pp. 5 top right, 27, 33, 39, 40 © AP Images; pp. 7, 13, 21, 26, 34 Shutterstock; p. 8 Rod Mikinski; pp. 9, 19, 25, 30 © www.istockphotos.com/Todd Bates; p. 18 © Shelly Castellano/Icon SMI/Corbis; pp. 22, 36 University of Texas; p. 40 © Icon SMI.

Designer: Tom Forget
Photo Researcher: Marty Levick